C000124560

Acknowledgements

This book has been written as a small contribution towards giving all children access to the financial education they need to get on the money ladder.

I'd like to say thank you to my Rach & Patel families for their support and help in making this come to life.

I'd also like to say thanks to my colleagues at FTAdviser for their support.

The FT has not seen or endorsed the content of this book.

LOOSE CHANGE

-TINA LEARNS TO SAVE-

BY SONIA RACH

Tina and her mum were getting ready to go to the supermarket to do their weekly shopping.

"Are you ready to go?", Mum asked.

"Yes Mum- I'll be down in a few minutes," shouted Tina.

Tina was counting her pocket money to see how much she had managed to save up.

"Mum, I've managed to save up £25 now!" said Tina very excitedly.

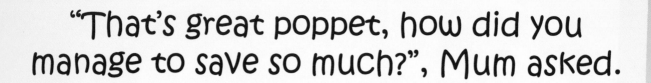

"That's great poppet, how did you manage to save so much?", Mum asked.

"Well I have the birthday money from Grandpa and Nana, plus the extra chores I did," Tina said.

"Mum, can I take it with me to the supermarket and spend it?"
"There's a new toy I really want!"

"Of course you can," Mum said.

"Mummy, please can I use my pocket money to buy this new toy?" Tina said.

"I think I've saved up enough and I promise to share it when I play!"

"Sure, you can buy it, but what will you do with the change?" asked Mum.

Tina was confused by her mum's question.

"Change? What's that?" she said.

"The toy is £15, and you have £25," Mum said.

"£25 - £15 = £10. "So, once you pay for the toy, you will receive £10 back. The money left over is known as 'CHANGE'."

£25 - £15 = £10

"Oh wow," Tina thought.
"So, what can I buy with £10?
Maybe some sweets?"

Excited that she would have money left over, Tina ran around the supermarket trying to see what she could buy for £10.

There were so many options. A few packs of biscuits, plus some sweets were only coming to £6.

"£10 - £6 = £4," Tina said. "So, I still have money left over!"

"Yes dear, you do but there are many things you can do with your £10 if you don't want to spend it," Mum said.

"Like what?" asked Tina.

"Well, you could keep it in your piggy bank and add more of your pocket money until you can afford to buy another toy," Mum said.

"That way you will be spending it on something you really want."

"Or, you can get more money added without doing anything – this is something called "EARNING INTEREST" on it."

"Interest?" said Tina. "What's that?"

Tina was confused by what her mum was
saying, how can I have more money
just by saving it.
"Where does the extra money come from?"

"Let me explain," Mum said.
"Money is something you can use to buy or sell something",

"Normally it's a product - like bread, milk or a toy - or a service like when we get a taxi to go somewhere."

"So where is all the money kept?"
Tina asked.
"On that plastic card you use?"

"Kind of," Mum said.

"Just like you use your piggy bank to keep your money safe, grown-ups use these places called banks."

"Our money is in the bank and then we use it to buy things."

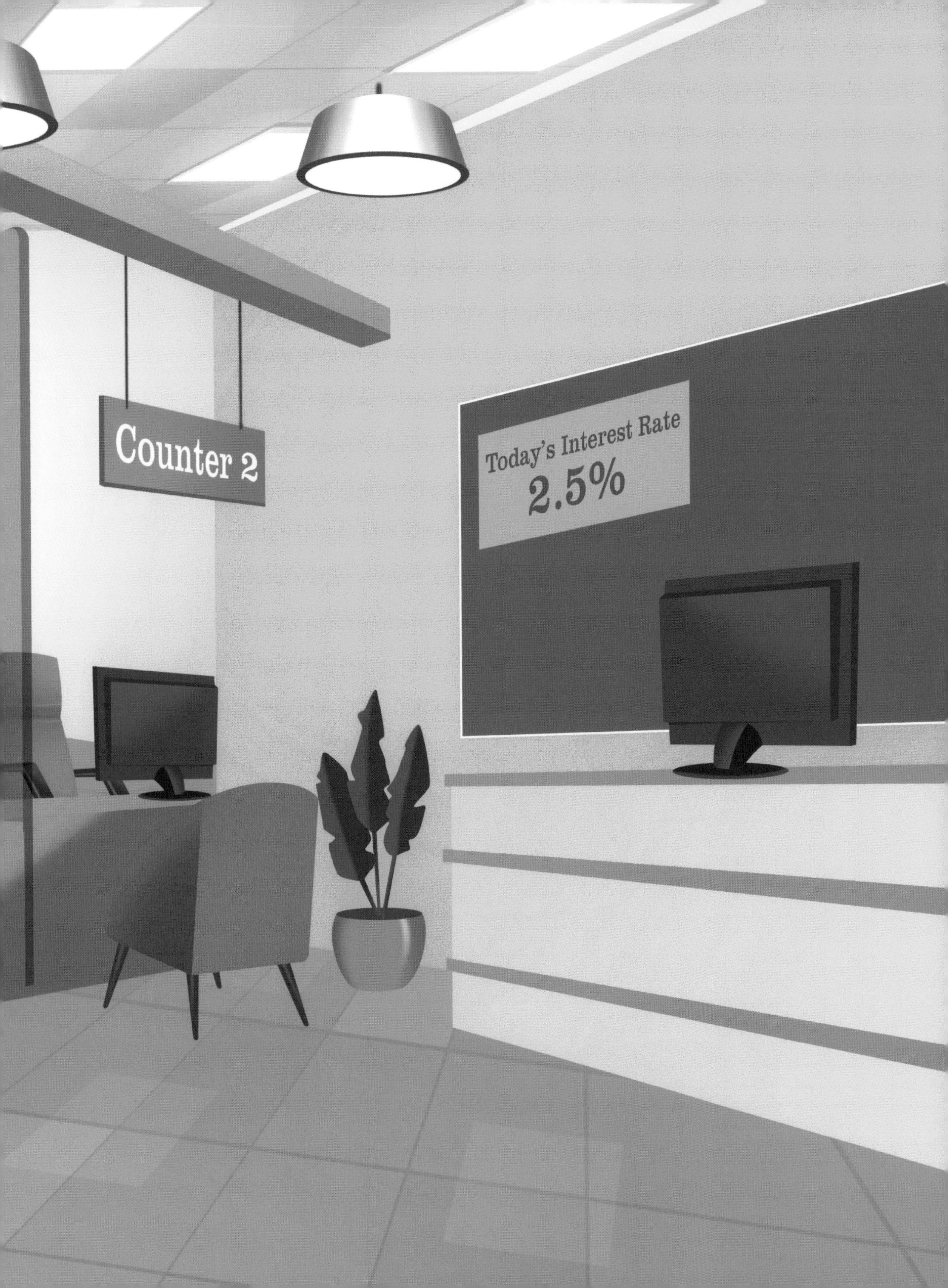
Counter 2
Today's Interest Rate
2.5%

"Wait, so I get free money without even doing any extra chores?" Tina said.

"That sounds amazing," she thought. "But how does it work?"

"Imagine you have 10 sweets," Mum said.

"For every day you don't eat it, I will give you an extra 3 sweets to add to the 10 as a reward for saving it."

"Like the sweets example, if I have £10 and I put it in the bank, will they add interest to this amount?", Tina asked.

"Exactly!" Mum said.

"So they will give me an extra 30p every month as a reward for keeping money there," Tina said.

"Mum this sounds incredible, imagine how many toys I can buy with that!

"But can kids like me put money in bank accounts?" asked Tina.

"Yes, there are kid-friendly accounts available where we can put your weekly £10 if you like," Mum said.

"Or you can give the change that you
want to save to me and dad
and I will add the interest for you."

"That's fantastic!
So when I get the weekly £10, can I
give you £5 to save and
add interest to and then I have £5 to
spend if I want to?" said Tina.

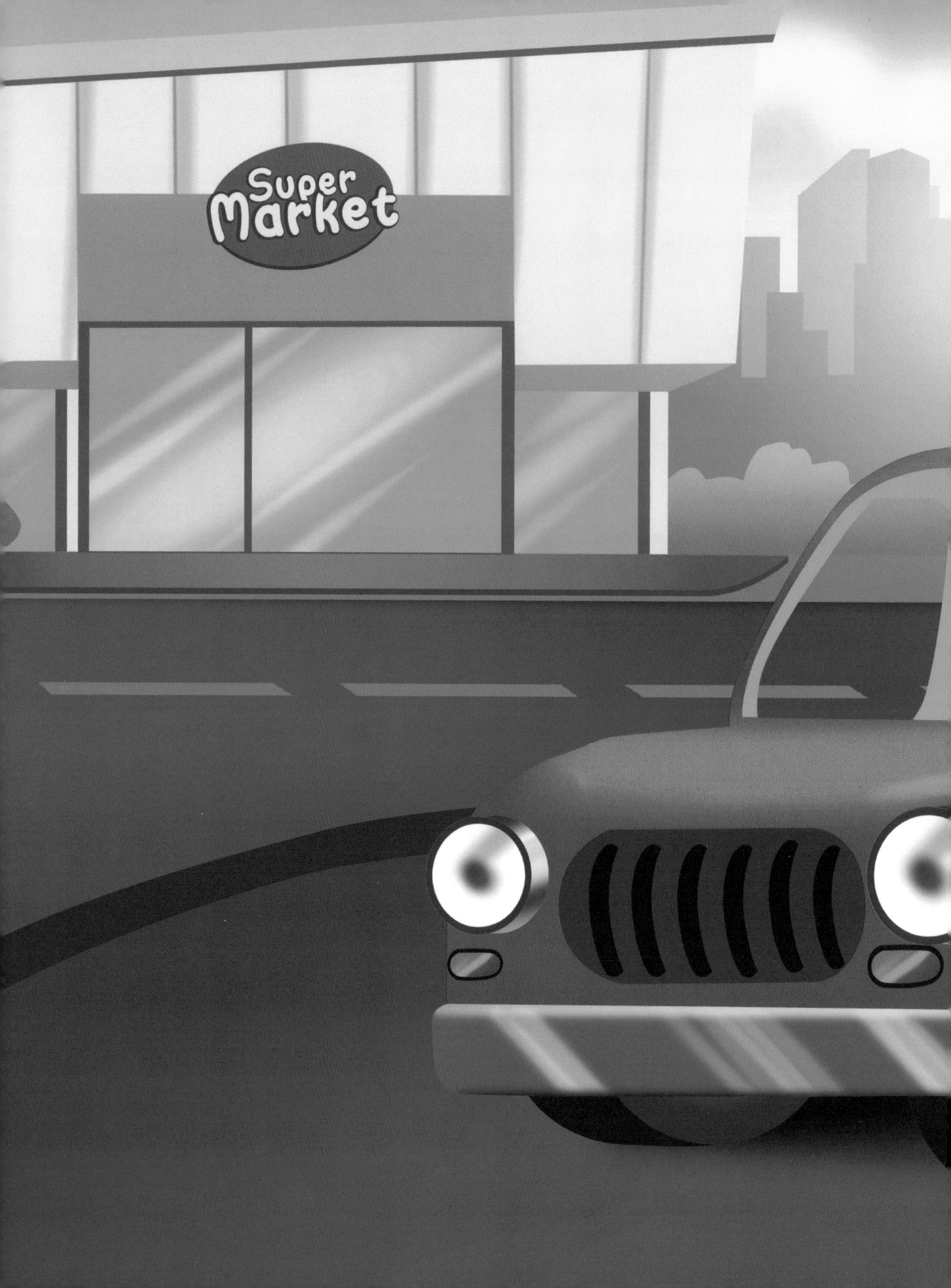
Super
Market

"Of course, you can!"

Tina was really excited thinking about all the extra toys she could buy JUST by saving her LOOSE CHANGE.

KEY TAKEAWAYS

Remember, it's important to be wise with your money.

Where do grown-ups keep their money?

What is an interest rate?

Why is it a good idea to save money and gain interest?

KEY TAKEAWAYS

S is for Saving money

A is for Amount - how much pocket money can I save?

V is for Value - is the reward more valuable or the item?

I is for Interest added to my savings

N is for Necessary - do I really need this?

G is for Grateful and being happy with what you have

Printed in Great Britain
by Amazon

32294698R00034